here often?

&

Other Proven Chat up Lines
By Christine Green

Published in the UK by
POWERFRESH Limited
21 Rothersthorpe Crescent
Northampton
NN4 8JD

Telephone   0845 130 4565
Facsimile   0845 130 4563
E Mail   info@powerfresh.co.uk

ISBN   190292973X

Printed in Malta by Gutenberg Press Ltd
Powerfresh September 2003

Do you have problems when it comes to chatting up a member of the opposite sex (or even your own sex) then take a look through this collection of tried and tested 'chat up lines' and you'll have them falling at your knees! But don't blame me if they don't work remember, there is a time and a place, just pick both carefully!

**Playing games can always
be a turn on.**

Have you ever played leapfrog
naked?

Some games can be more exciting than others

Have you ever played 'Spank the Brunette?'

But remember there is always a time and a place

Let's play Titanic when I say 'Iceberg, you go down.

You could always suggest a party, you don't need many guests

Why don't you and me have a party and invite your pants to come on down

Doctors and Nurses is for kids

Hey baby, let's play house, you can be the door and I'll slam you!

Make the invitation sound exciting

Imagine this, you, me bubble bath and a huge magnum of the best champagne

But don't expect a reward in return.

If I gave you a sexy black negligee would there be anything in it for me?

Add humour when introducing yourself

Hi. My name is Milk. I'll do your body good.

What girl couldn't resist this chat up, even if it does sound a little corny?

My friends and I voted you the most beautiful woman in the room and the prize is me

Tell them your secret dream

I keep having wet dreams, would
you like to make them reality?

Make them feel precious

I want to melt in your mouth, not in your hand

Be original

I've got the ship; you've got the harbour what d'you say we tie up for the night?

Be passionate

Lie down, I think I love you

But before getting down to any serious business...

Pardon me but are you a screamer or a moaner?

Some women/men like the intelligent approach

Did you realise, there are 265 bones in the human body. How would you like just one more?

And remember, no pressure

So what are the chances that we
can engage in anything more than
just conversation?

Always be a 'gent'

Why don't you come and sit on my lap then we can talk about the first thing that pops up.

Don't get too personal too quickly

Hey I'm looking for treasure. Can I look around your chest?

And go easy when talking about what they're wearing

That belt looks very tight. Would you like me to loosen it for you?

Often a question can result in a date

Do you live on a chicken farm?
Hopefully the girl will say no
Well there's one thing you sure
know how to raise cocks.

**Don't let anything stand in
the path of true passion**

Let's only Latex stand between our
love

Question with a number

Pick a number between 1 and 10.
Shit you lose now take off your
clothes.

Girls like to made genuine promises

You look cold. Tell you what let me be your electric blanket. Just plug me in and I'll make you feel nice and toasty inside and out.

Offer them something special

You know what they say about
guys with big hands
(*Hopefully girl will reply*)
'No, what do they say?
Big latex

And whilst on the subject of offering them something

I'm like a Domino's Pizza, if you don't cum in 30 minutes the next one is free

Always leave them wondering

Girls find my really sexy because I rarely wear any underwear and when I do it's generally something erotically exotic... Would you like to see?

But don't forget that sensitive, caring side of your nature

Can I offer you nine inches of strength and sensitivity?

But don't go over the top

Know the difference between a
chicken leg and my penis?
Hopefully the girl will reply, "No"
Fancy going back to my place and
find out

**And never make a promise
you can't fulfil**

I promise baby, when I deliver, it'll
make you shiver

Don't let on you are obsessed with sex

Do you believe that guys really think with their dick?
(No doubt girl will reply) Yeah
Well in that case will you blow mine?

Never waste time

Since we shouldn't waste this time
and day I think we ought to use
these condoms in my pocket before
they expire

And don't confound her with figures

What do you say if we go back to my place and so some maths? Add a bed, subtract out clothes and divide your legs and multiply.

Of course some guys never beat about the bush but come straight out with it

Hi, I always have sex on the first date, what about you?

Whilst others go another way around asking for sex

You know if I were you I'd have sex with me

It doesn't mean that the pub is closing that the night is over

Shame that happy hour is over but it's still going strong at my place

There are the odd occasions when a certain job can come in very useful providing you can say it with a straight face

I'm conducting a survey on the taste of vaginas. Would you like to be my first participant?

**Every woman loves a man
with a different pick up line**

Would you like to try an Australian
kiss? It's just like a French one but
down under.

And for the downright show off

Hey I'll fuck you so well the neighbours will be having a cigarette when we're done

Some fellas and girls don't even need asking

Let's face it. I'm hot you're hot and we both know you've got a crush on me. And really who can blame you with a gorgeous face like this. So can I snatch a kiss or I don't mind.

Dead corny but it could well work on the right person

I feel like Richard Gere when I'm standing next to you, the Pretty Woman

A dead cert chat up for the bumptious type

I wish I were that outfit because then I could wear you out

And one for the gentle

Do you really taste as good as you
smell?

For the cocky one

Hi my name is Mr Right; someone
said you were looking for me

**And the downright
egotistical one**

Nice legs what time do they open?

Young fellas always try this one

Excuse me but I'm doing a report on stamina. Would you be interested in finding the true meaning of a marathon?

Good chat up line for the Hungry Farmer

I'd like to wrap your legs around my head and wear you like a feedbag

One way to confuse a girl

If it's true that we are what we eat,
I could be you by morning

Might need to be slightly inebriated to get away with this one

I was about to go and masturbate and I needed a name to go with your face.

For the budding poet who obviously doesn't know it

Roses are red, Violets are blue.
I like spaghetti lets go screw

Which one is worst?

Roses are Red Apples are sour.
I'll spread my legs and you can
show me your power

For the cheeky boy/girl

Could I touch your belly button...
from the inside?

Some chat ups could put you off your favourite foods

Come on baby, sex is like pizza:
Even if it's bad, it's still pretty good.

This chat up is definitely worth considering

Do you wanna have kids with
me???
No?
Okay, then do you just wanna
practice?

Nice chat up for the 'DIY' store

I'm gonna have to put you on my 'To Do' List

Who could refuse to answer this question?

The only thing your eyes haven't told me is your name

Not a line for those who easily get tongue twisted

Excuse me but I just noticed you noticing me and I just wanted to give you notice that I noticed you too.

This one sounds more like a sleep over than a pop over to my place

So how do you like your eggs: poached, scrambled or how about fertilized

But what is a chat up without some back chat

Man - Would you like to dance?

Woman - I don't like this song and I certainly wouldn't dance with you

The old ones always sound the best

Man - 'Scuse me but is this seat empty?

Woman - Yes and so will this one be if you sit down

Try staying clear of invitations

Man - Your place or mine

Woman – Both. You go to your place and I'll go to mine

There is always a question of their current employment

Man – So what do you do for a living?

Woman – I'm a female impersonator, what line are you in sweetie

Even if it isn't always what you wanted to hear

**Be prepared, most women
are on the ball**

Man - Hey baby what's your
sign?

Woman - Do not enter

The old ones are always the best ones

Man - Haven't I seen you someplace before

Woman - Yes that's why I don't go there anymore

A lapse of memory is always a good move in the right direction

Fuck me if I'm wrong but is your name Gertrude

What is it they say in the movie business? 'Never work with kids or animals'

I've lost my puppy don't suppose you've got time to help me find him. I think he went into this motel room down the road

Remember the war?

Want to play Pearl Harbour? You
remember it's a game where I lie
back while you blow the hell out of
me

You could always offer to buy a drink

I would buy you a drink but I would be jealous of the glass

This could raise a smile

I am fighting the urge to make you
the happiest woman on earth
tonight

Find out what they believe in

Are you by any chance religious?
They will either say yes or no
Because I could well be the answer
to your prayers

Always be upfront with those chat up lines

Do you know what people are saying behind your back? Nice ass

Be an open book

What smiles, winks, is hung like a
horse and can last all night long?
Then smile and wink.

**If you are keen on getting
them to talk to you**

I'm sorry for staring but you look
like someone I used to know

Be a born again flirt

Shall we talk or continue flirting
from a distance

Try a game of 'I-Spy'

There must be something wrong
with my eyes because I simply
can't take them off you.

This is sure to get a response

My drink is getting lonely would
you like to join me?

This could be taken in one of two ways

I never knew Barbie Dolls came fully-grown

Fashion conscious gurus this is certainly one for them

Is it a coincidence that your blouse matches my bedspread?

A pick up line with repercussions

I'd really like to see how you look when I'm naked

Could even be sung

I'd walk a million miles for one of your smiles and even further for that thing you do with your tongue.

Sounds so romantic

If you were the last woman and I were the last man on earth, we could do it in public

Cool customer to say this one

Baby, I'm an American Express lover and you really shouldn't go home without me.

Sure to tug at the heart strings

I really miss my Teddy Bear.
Would you sleep with me?

Memories

You remind me of a compass
because I'd be totally lost without
you

Cheeky, but cute

You see my friend over there. Well he wants to know if you think I'm cute.

Getting slightly near the knuckle

Have you ever seen a girl swallow an entire banana? (*Wink wink*)

There is of course always the old tried and tested chat up lines

Do you come here often? You could, with me

90

If all the old cliches fail

Will you marry me for an hour?

And there is always what goes on behind closed doors?

I've got a pimple on my butt, d'you want to see it?

Shower her with compliments

You have pretty eyeballs. Of course they'd be better if they were eyeing up my pretty balls.

If she is your type why hang around

You look my type of woman: nice hair, beautiful eyes, amazing body but there is still just one problem, your clothes
The girl will perhaps reply, What's wrong with them?
That's just it they're still on

If all else fails get right down to it

I can't think of a single line but I just wanted to talk to you

You can order other Little books directly from Powerfresh Limited. All at £2.50 each including postage (UK only)

Postage and packing outside the UK: Europe: add 20% of retail price
Rest of the world: add 30% of retail price
To order any Powerfresh book please call 0845 130 4565
Powerfresh Limited 21 Rothersthorpe Crescent Northampton NN4 8JD